The NatureTrail Book of BIRDWATCHING

Malcolm Hart

Identifying Birds with this book

This book is about common European birds you can see. It tells you how they live and also shows you how to find them. When you see a bird, and you want to know its name, or more about it, use this book as follows:

Turn to the back of the book (pages 28–31) and look it up in the section called **Common Birds to Spot.** If you can't see a picture of it there . . .

Turn to the page in the book which deals with the **kind of place** where you saw it. For example, pages 18–19 tell you about birds that live in woodlands and forests.

If you still can't find it, look on other pages of the book, such as pages 10–11 which show you what birds you can attract to your garden. Always make careful notes about birds you see and try to identify them later.

USBORNE

Mistle Thrush

Nuthatch

Siskin

Written by
Malcolm Hart

Series Editor
Sue Jacquemier

Consultant Editor
Peter Holden,
National Organiser of the
Young Ornithologists' Club

Designed by
Mike Ricketts

Assistant Editor
Jane Stephenson

Illustrated by
Dave Ashby, Hilary Burn,
The Garden Studio, Colin
King, Ken Lilly, Linden
Artists, Richard Millington,
Charles Pearson, Gillian
Platt, Maurice Pledger,
Mike Ricketts

Printed in Belgium by
Henri Proost, Turnhout,
Belgium.

First published in 1976 by
Usborne Publishing Ltd,
20 Garrick Street,
London WC2
Text and Artwork © 1976 by
Usborne Publishing Ltd.

The NatureTrail Book of BIRDWATCHING

About This Book

This book tells you where to look for common European birds and how best to study them. It shows you some clues to look for, how birds live in different kinds of places, and how to collect information.

Contents

How to be a Birdwatcher 4
What to Look for 6
Clues and Tracks 8
Making a Bird Garden 10
Making a Nesting Box 12
The Nesting Season 14

Places to Look for Birds
Ponds and Inland
   Waterways 16
Woodlands and Forests 18
Towns and Cities 20
Sea Coasts 22
Mountains and
   Moorlands 24
Migrating Birds 26

Common Birds to Spot
Sparrow- and Blackbird-
   sized Birds 28
Crow- and Mallard-
   sized Birds 30
Larger Birds 31

Bearded
Reedlings

Stonechat

How to be a Birdwatcher

The most important thing for any birdwatcher to have is a notebook. It is difficult to keep all the facts in your head and if you try you will probably forget some important points.

Try to keep any notes you make clear and readable. The picture shows how to set your notebook out. Try to draw the birds you see. Even a bad drawing is better than nothing.

When you get home, look up the bird you have seen in this book.

A birdwatcher has to take notes quickly. Use a spiralbound notebook like the one here. It has a stiff back to help you write easily. File your notes away in date order when you get home. When you are out, keep your book in a plastic bag to keep it dry.

Male Reed Bunting

Look for the shape and obvious marks first. The Reed Bunting has a sparrow-like body, a dark head, white collar and white outer tail feathers.

Black Head
White collar
2nd August 1975
Weather sunny
Canon Hill Park
M Reed Bunting
Grey-white underneath
Dark Brown Streaked Back
Flight Pattern
Also F carrying grass (for * ?)

Make sure you have all the details of place, date, and weather entered in your notebook.

How does the bird fly? Make a drawing of the sort of flight it has, and note where it goes.

Bird Shorthand

M   = MALE
F   = FEMALE
JUV = JUVENILE (YOUNG BIRD NOT IN ADULT FEATHERS)
✱   = NEST
C10 = ABOUT TEN (WHEN TALKING ABOUT NUMBERS OF BIRDS)

Use these signs instead of writing out the words—it will save you time. Take two pencils with you.

How to Stalk Birds

CAMOUFLAGE YOUR SHAPE BY STANDING IN FRONT OF OR BEHIND A TREE OR BUSH. YOUR DULL CLOTHES WILL BLEND IN WITH THE BACKGROUND. KEEP THE SUN BEHIND, SO THAT YOU ARE IN SHADOW AND THE BIRD IS IN SUNLIGHT

IF THERE IS NO COVER, CRAWL CLOSER USING YOUR ELBOWS AND FEET. DON'T WEAR CLOTHES THAT RUSTLE WHEN YOU MOVE. NEVER MAKE QUICK MOVEMENTS IN THE OPEN

What to Wear

Hat or hood (remember to wear dull colours)

Travel as light as possible

Binoculars

Anorak or warm coat

Notebook and pencils

One or two pairs of socks

Trousers tucked into wellingtons

Buying Binoculars

The best size to get is 7 × 50 or 8 × 30

Choose the lightest pair you can find

Binoculars are not essential for the beginner, but if you want some, go to a shop with someone who knows about binoculars, and try several pairs to see how they feel.

HOWEVER LIGHT YOUR BINOCULARS ARE, THEY WILL START TO FEEL HEAVY AFTER A WHILE. TO TAKE THE WEIGHT OFF YOUR NECK, TIE SOME STRING ONTO THE STRAP AS SHOWN

Binocular strap

String tied to strap and belt

Belt

Quick Field Sketches

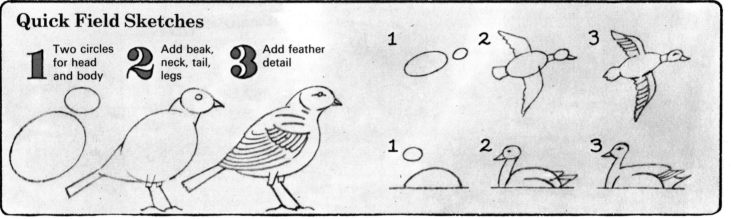

1 Two circles for head and body

2 Add beak, neck, tail, legs

3 Add feather detail

The best way to take notes on the birds you see is to draw quick sketches of them. Begin by drawing two circles—one for the body and one for the head. Notice the size and position of the head and body before you start. Then add the tail, beak and legs. Fill in the details of the feathers if you have time. Practise drawing the birds you can see from your window first.

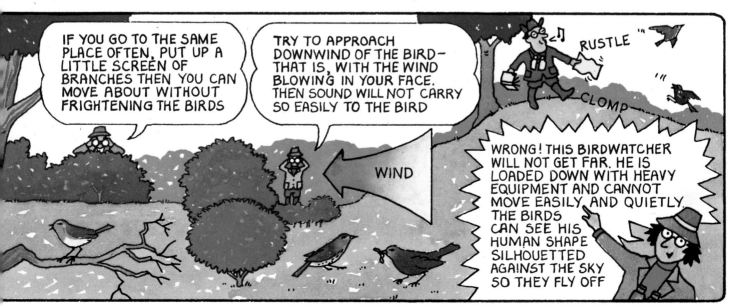

IF YOU GO TO THE SAME PLACE OFTEN, PUT UP A LITTLE SCREEN OF BRANCHES THEN YOU CAN MOVE ABOUT WITHOUT FRIGHTENING THE BIRDS

TRY TO APPROACH DOWNWIND OF THE BIRD— THAT IS, WITH THE WIND BLOWING IN YOUR FACE. THEN SOUND WILL NOT CARRY SO EASILY TO THE BIRD

WIND

RUSTLE

CLOMP

WRONG! THIS BIRDWATCHER WILL NOT GET FAR. HE IS LOADED DOWN WITH HEAVY EQUIPMENT AND CANNOT MOVE EASILY AND QUIETLY. THE BIRDS CAN SEE HIS HUMAN SHAPE SILHOUETTED AGAINST THE SKY SO THEY FLY OFF

What to Look for

These pages tell you what to look for when you want to identify a bird. When you see a bird for the first time, there are several questions you should ask. What size is it? Compare it with a bird you know like a Sparrow or a Blackbird.

Has it any obvious marks like the Reed Bunting's black head and white outer tail feathers? How does it fly and feed? How does it behave? Where is it? What colour is it? Some differences in colour can be confusing: there are some examples opposite.

A female Sparrowhawk chasing a male Reed Bunting. The labels give examples of the kind of things to note down when you see a bird.

Rounded wings

Black head

White collar

Hooked beak

White outer tail feathers

Long tail feathers

Yellow legs

Flight Patterns

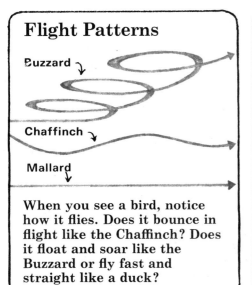

Buzzard

Chaffinch

Mallard

When you see a bird, notice how it flies. Does it bounce in flight like the Chaffinch? Does it float and soar like the Buzzard or fly fast and straight like a duck?

Shapes in Flight

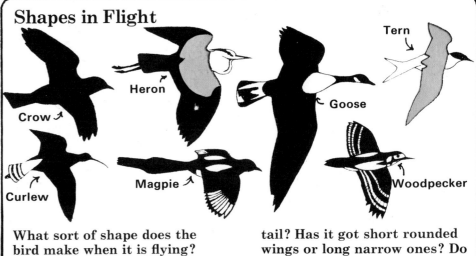

Tern

Heron

Crow

Goose

Curlew

Magpie

Woodpecker

What sort of shape does the bird make when it is flying? Has it a long or short neck or tail? Has it got short rounded wings or long narrow ones? Do its feet stick out behind its tail?

Sex Differences

Male
Female
Blackbirds

The males of some birds, like the Blackbird, have different coloured feathers and beaks from the females.

Colour Changes

Summer
Winter
Black-Headed Gulls

Some birds, like the Black-Headed Gull, have a different plumage in winter from the one they have in summer.

Age Differences

Adult
Juvenile (Young)
Robins

In some birds, like the Robin, the young look very different from their parents.

Looking at Beaks

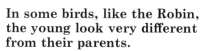
Curlew

Carrion Crow
Greenfinch
Heron

Beaks can give you clues to what a bird eats. The Crow's beak is a general-purpose tool. The Greenfinch's beak is more suited to eating seeds. The Curlew uses its long beak for probing for food in mud and the Heron uses its beak for catching fish.

> ONE WAY TO IDENTIFY A BIRD IS FROM ITS SONG. GO OUT WITH SOMEONE WHO KNOWS BIRD SONG WELL, OR BORROW RECORDS OF BIRD SONG FROM YOUR LOCAL LIBRARY

Watch What Birds are Doing

Grey Wagtail

The Wagtail often patrols in mud or short grass. It wags its tail up and down. Sometimes it makes a dash after an insect.

Treecreeper

The treecreeper creeps around tree trunks, picking out insects from the bark with its thin, curved bill.

Turnstone

The turnstone walks along the beach turning over seaweed and stones, looking for small creatures to eat.

Clues and Tracks

Sometimes you can tell which birds have been in an area by the clues that they leave behind. After some practice these are easy to recognize. Their feathers and the remains of meals are the ones you will see most often.

You may not be able to identify the feathers you find straight away. But later you may find a dead bird or see a bird in a zoo or museum that has feathers like the ones you have collected. Remember that most birds have feathers of many different colours and sizes.

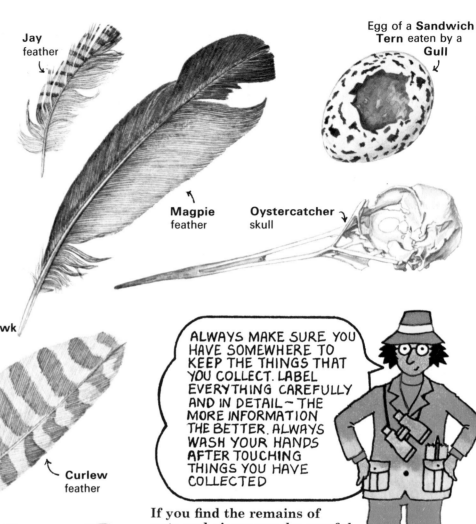

Jay feather

Magpie feather

Egg of a **Sandwich Tern** eaten by a **Gull**

Oystercatcher skull

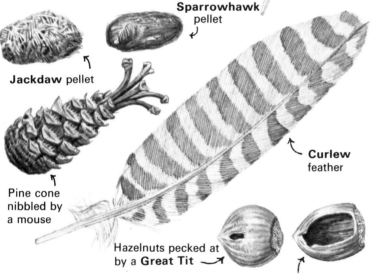

Jackdaw pellet

Sparrowhawk pellet

Pine cone nibbled by a mouse

Curlew feather

Hazelnuts pecked at by a **Great Tit**

and by a **Woodpecker**

ALWAYS MAKE SURE YOU HAVE SOMEWHERE TO KEEP THE THINGS THAT YOU COLLECT. LABEL EVERYTHING CAREFULLY AND IN DETAIL — THE MORE INFORMATION THE BETTER. ALWAYS WASH YOUR HANDS AFTER TOUCHING THINGS YOU HAVE COLLECTED

If you find the remains of nuts and pinecones, be careful how you identify the creatures that have been eating them, as these things are the food of squirrels and mice, as well as of birds.

Collecting Feathers and Wings

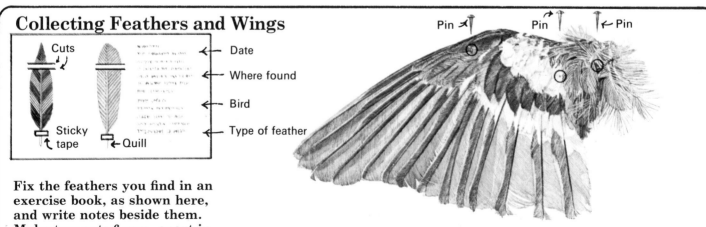

Cuts

Sticky tape

Quill

Date

Where found

Bird

Type of feather

Pin

Pin

Pin

Fix the feathers you find in an exercise book, as shown here, and write notes beside them. Make two cuts 6 mm. apart in the page. Thread the feather through and stick the quill down with tape.

Wings cut from dead birds can be dried and kept. Pin the wing out on a piece of stiff board. It

should dry in a few days and can then be placed in an envelope with a label and some mothballs.

Pinecones

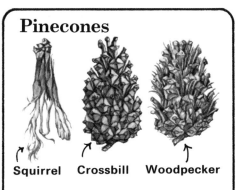

Squirrel Crossbill Woodpecker

Here are three examples of pinecones that have been attacked by birds or animals. They break open the cones in different ways to search for seeds.

Nuts

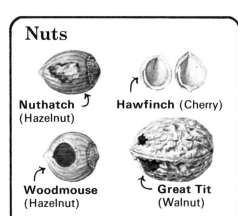

Nuthatch (Hazelnut)

Hawfinch (Cherry)

Woodmouse (Hazelnut)

Great Tit (Walnut)

Animals all have their own ways of opening nuts. Mice chew neat little holes while birds leave jagged holes or split the nuts in half.

The Thrush's Anvil

Snail shell

Anvil

Broken shells

Song Thrushes use stones to break open snail shells. Look for the thrush's "anvil"—it will be surrounded by the remains of the bird's meal.

Owl Pellets

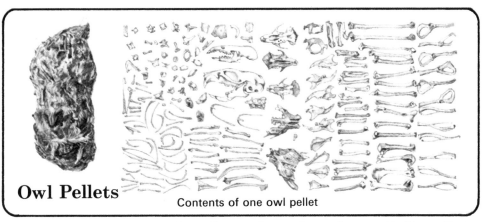

Contents of one owl pellet

Owls swallow small animals and birds whole, and then cough up the fur, feathers and bones as a pellet. You can find these beneath trees or posts where the owl rests. Pull a pellet apart and sort out the bones. The easiest to identify are the skulls of animals which the owl has eaten.

Other Pellets

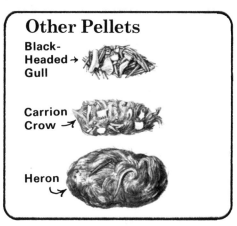

Black-Headed Gull

Carrion Crow

Heron

Many birds other than owls produce pellets. But it is harder to identify what is in them as most other birds do not eat large enough animals.

1 Footprint Casts

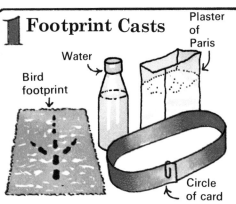

Plaster of Paris

Water

Bird footprint

Circle of card

To make plaster casts you will need water, plaster of Paris, a beaker and a strip of card bent into a circle, and held by a paperclip.

2

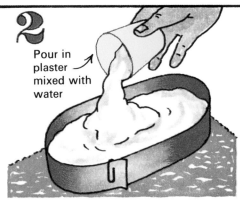

Pour in plaster mixed with water

Put the card around the footprint. Mix the plaster, pour it into the circle and let it harden. Wrap the cast in tissues and take it home.

3

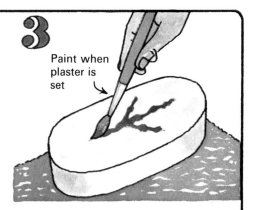

Paint when plaster is set

Wash off any dirt. Leave the cast for a few days and then carefully remove it from the card. Paint the footprint and then varnish it.

Making a Bird Garden

This picture shows many of the birds that visit gardens or window-sills for food. Different kinds of food attract different birds. Put out bones, suet, cheese, oats, peanuts, sunflower seeds, currants and bits of bacon rind. Scatter food in the open for birds that prefer to eat on the ground, and build a bird bath.

Key to Birds

1 Greenfinch	8 Chaffinch
2 House Sparrow	9 Blackbird
3 Blue Tit	10 Mistle Thrush
4 Great Tit	11 Goldfinch
5 Robin	12 Song Thrush
6 Coal Tit	13 Dunnock
7 Starling	14 Bullfinch

REMEMBER :- DON'T ATTRACT BIRDS TO A SPOT WHERE YOU KNOW CATS ARE LURKING. DON'T STOP FEEDING BIRDS SUDDENLY IN WINTER – THEY RELY ON YOUR FOOD SUPPLY AND MAY STARVE IF THEY CANNOT FIND FOOD ELSEWHERE

Feeding Chart

	CHEESE	BACON	NUTS
BLUE TIT	✓	✓✓✓	✓✓✓✓
ROBIN			
STARLING			
BLACKBIRD			

Make a chart of the kinds of food you see different birds eating. Which birds like nuts best? Tick the boxes each time you see the bird eat something.

Plants That Birds Like to Eat

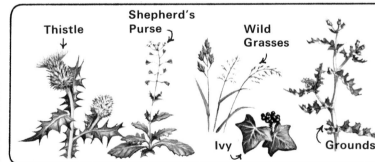

Thistle
Shepherd's Purse
Wild Grasses
Ivy
Grounds

All these plants are good bird food. If you have a garden try to let a little patch grow wild. Weeds like Thistles, Groundsel and Shepherd's Purse have seeds that birds like to eat. Trees and bushes like Hawthorn, Cotoneaster, Rowan and Elder have lots of good berries in the autumn. Some birds like over-ripe apples and sultanas. Dig

Putting out Food

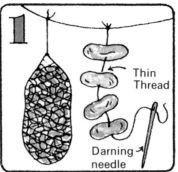

Melt the fat in a warm oven

Matchstick

Darning needle

Thin Thread

Darning needle

Yoghurt pot

Supermarkets often sell vegetables in nets. Fill one of these with unsalted peanuts, or thread peanuts on a string, and hang them up.

To make a feeding bell with a yoghurt pot, fill the pot with a mixture of breadcrumbs, currants, cooked (not raw) potato and oatmeal. Pour on

some melted fat and wait until it hardens before you hang the feeder up. Tits and Finches will be able to cling on and feed.

Make a Bird Table

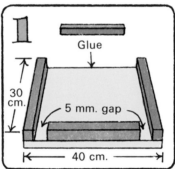

Glue

30 cm.

5 mm. gap

40 cm.

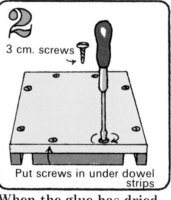

3 cm. screws

Put screws in under dowel strips

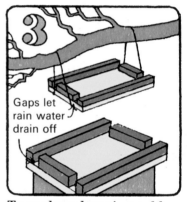

Gaps let rain water drain off

You will need a piece of outdoor quality plywood about 40 cm. × 30 cm., and four strips of dowel, each about 30 cm. long. Glue the dowel to the plywood.

When the glue has dried, turn the table over and put in two screws on every side as shown. Protect your table with a wood preservative and screw it to a box or tub.

To make a hanging table, put four screw-eyes into the sides and hang it from a branch. Clean the table regularly with disinfectant.

Make a Bird Bath

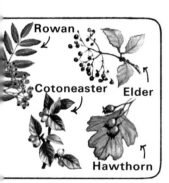

Rowan

Cotoneaster   Elder

Hawthorn

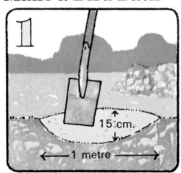

15 cm.

1 metre

Make sure polythene has no tears

over a patch of earth to make it easier for Blackbirds and Thrushes to find worms and insects.

Choose a place not too close to the feeding area. Dig a hole with sloping sides about 15 cm. deep and one metre wide. Dig from the middle outwards.

Line the hole with a piece of strong polythene (a dustbin liner will do). Weight the plastic down with stones and sprinkle gravel or sand over the lining.

Put a few stones and a short branch in the middle of the bath to make a perch. Fill the bath with water. Keep it full (and ice-free in winter).

Making a Nesting Box

You can encourage birds to come to your garden in spring by building them a nesting box. If the entrance hole is small a Blue Tit is the bird most likely to nest in the box. If it is larger you may find a House Sparrow using it. Other birds, like Great Tits, Starlings, Tree Sparrows, Nuthatches and even Wrens sometimes use nesting boxes. You can look inside your box but try not to disturb the birds. You can always watch them from indoors.

> TO MAKE YOUR NESTING BOX YOU WILL NEED SOME PLYWOOD THAT IS 12 MM THICK. EITHER GET THE WOOD CUT TO SIZE AT THE SHOP OR ASK AN ADULT TO SAW IT FOR YOU

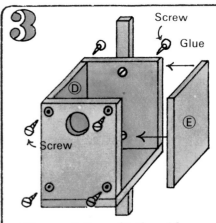

Side Ⓔ removed to show how box is made

How to Cut the Wood

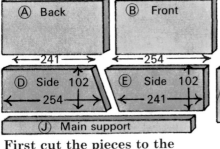

Ⓐ Back
Ⓑ Front
Base Ⓒ
Waste
←— 241 —→
←— 254 —→
Ⓓ Side 102
←— 254 —→
Ⓔ Side 102
←— 241 —→
Battens
Top Ⓕ
Ⓖ Ⓗ
Waste
Ⓙ Main support

First cut the pieces to the following sizes:

A 254 mm. × 127 mm.
B 241 mm. × 127 mm.
C 127 mm. × 127 mm.
D 241 mm. × 102 mm.
E 254 mm. × 102 mm.
F 152 mm. × 127 mm.

G 102 mm. × 25 mm.
H 102 mm. × 25 mm.
J 510 mm. × 25 mm.

Overall length: 915 mm.
Overall width: 254 mm.

50 mm.

Drill the entrance hole with a hand drill about 50 mm. from the top of the front section. The hole should be 25 mm. wide.

25 mm.

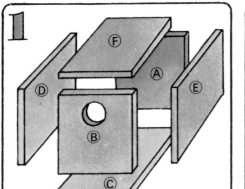

1 First arrange all the pieces to make sure that they fit together properly. Then drill holes for all the screws.

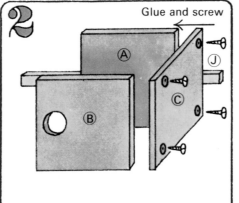

2 Glue and screw

Fix the main support onto the back with two screws. Glue and screw the bottom onto the back and then the front.

3 Screw

Glue

Glue and then fit the side pieces into place. Screw them on if they fit properly.

Where to Put the Box

Your completed box should be fixed to a tree or to an ivy-covered wall. The entrance hole should not face south or west as the heat from direct sunlight might kill the young birds. Fix it about two metres above the ground (away from cats). Empty out the old nest every winter, disinfect the box and give it a new coat of wood preservative before replacing it.

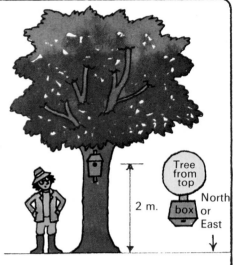

Keeping a Record

Try to make a note of what happens in your nesting box. You may even see some birds visiting the box in winter. They use boxes to sleep in. The notes below tell you the sort of thing to record.

1 Date of first visit.
2 Number of birds visiting.
3 Date bird first enters box.
4 Dates birds bring nest material.
5 Type of nest material.
6 Date birds first bring food.
7 Type of food.
8 Date young leave nest.

Other Types of Box

Special nesting boxes can be bought for House Martins. You can fix them under the edge of the roof.

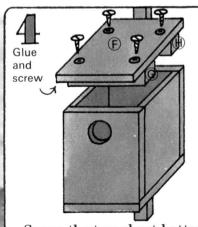

Screw the two short battens onto the top piece. Make sure the removable lid fits tightly.

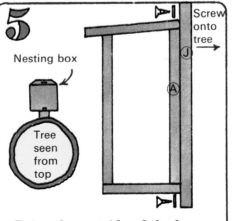

Paint the outside of the box with wood preservative and let it dry. Screw or nail it on to a tree (see above).

An open-fronted box can be made for other birds. It is like the nesting box shown opposite but the front panel is only 165 mm. high.

The Nesting Season

The nesting season is a time of great activity for all birds. First they have to find a place where they can build their nests and feed. This area then becomes their territory. When they have found a mate they have to build a nest, lay eggs and rear their young. With all this going on, it is not difficult to find out when and where a bird is building its nest or feeding its young. A bird carrying something in its beak is the most common sign. On these pages are some clues to help you.

Food Chart

Make a food chart to record which birds you see carrying

	WORMS	SNAILS	INSECTS
BLACK-BIRD			
ROBIN			
SONG-THRUSH			

food to their young, and the type of food.

The Song Thrush builds its nest in a bush. There are usually four or five eggs. Both parents feed the young birds with worms and snails.

REMEMBER~ IT IS AGAINST THE LAW TO DISTURB BREEDING BIRDS OR THEIR NESTS AND EGGS. BUT IF YOU ARE CAREFUL YOU CAN WATCH FROM A DISTANCE WITHOUT UPSETTING THEM AT ALL

The adult bird arrives at the nest with food. It pushes the food into the mouth of one of the young birds, removes any droppings from the nest and flies off to collect more food.

When a parent bird approaches the nest, the young birds beg for food with wide, open mouths.

Spotting Nesting Birds

Rook

Nightingale

Stonechat

Droppings

In the spring you will often see birds carrying nest material in their beaks. Rooks break off large twigs from trees for their nests.

Look out and listen for a bird singing in the same place every day during spring and summer. It is probably a sign that it is breeding.

You may see adult birds carrying droppings away from the nest in their beaks. They do this to keep the nest clean.

Nest Materials

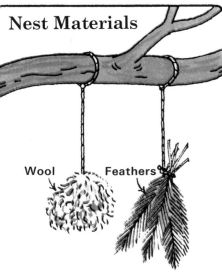

Wool   Feathers

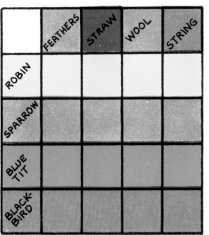

	FEATHERS	STRAW	WOOL	STRING
ROBIN				
SPARROW				
BLUE TIT				
BLACK-BIRD				

Hang up bits of wool, feathers, straw and string from a tree. Make a note of what different materials birds collect to use for their nests.

Where Birds Nest

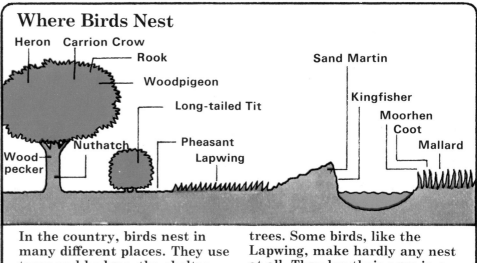

Heron   Carrion Crow
Rook
Woodpigeon
Long-tailed Tit
Sand Martin
Kingfisher
Moorhen
Coot
Mallard
Nuthatch
Pheasant
Lapwing
Wood-pecker

In the country, birds nest in many different places. They use trees and hedges, the shelter of steep banks and holes in trees. Some birds, like the Lapwing, make hardly any nest at all. They lay their eggs in a shallow hole in the ground.

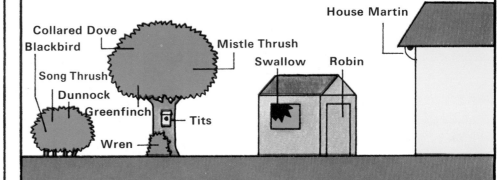

Collared Dove
Blackbird
Mistle Thrush
House Martin
Swallow   Robin
Song Thrush
Dunnock
Greenfinch
Tits
Wren

Many birds nest in gardens but only in sheltered places, safe from cats and dogs. They use thick bushes, trees, ivy-covered walls and sheds as well as nesting boxes. Some birds, like the House Martin, even build under the roof.

Ponds and Inland Waterways

Ducks are the birds you are most likely to see on a pond. They have quite long necks, webbed feet and wide, flat bills. They are all good swimmers. Most of them feed on the water weeds and plant life in the pond. There are three kinds of duck—the diving ducks, like the Tufted Duck, the dabblers, like the Mallard, that often up-end for their food and the rarer fish-eating ducks called Sawbills. Look out for other water birds like Swans, Geese, Moorhens and Coots.

Mallards are probably the commonest birds on the pond. The females (ducks) are much less colourful than the males. The correct word for a male duck is "drake".

Young Mallards

Male Mallard

Female Mallard

It uses its long, flat bill to sift the water for food.

Both male and female ducks have a blue flash on each wing called a speculum.

How Water Birds Feed

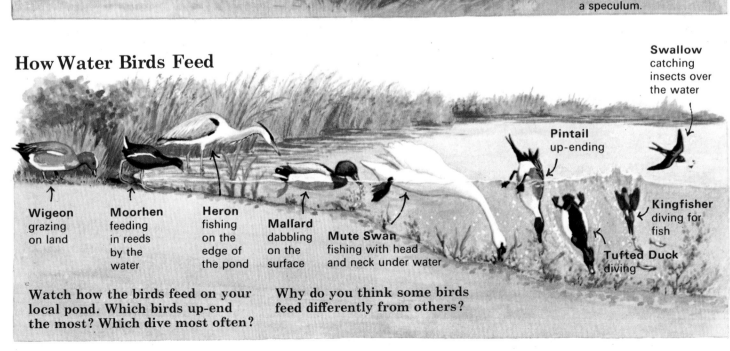

Swallow catching insects over the water

Pintail up-ending

Wigeon grazing on land

Moorhen feeding in reeds by the water

Heron fishing on the edge of the pond

Mallard dabbling on the surface

Mute Swan fishing with head and neck under water

Kingfisher diving for fish

Tufted Duck diving

Watch how the birds feed on your local pond. Which birds up-end the most? Which dive most often?

Why do you think some birds feed differently from others?

Taking-Off and Landing

Goldeneye

Most water birds are heavy, and have to work hard to get airborne. Many of them run over the surface, flapping their wings until they get up enough speed to take off. To land, they fly low over the water, with their feet sticking out to act as a brake.

Swimming

Shoveler

Coot

Moorhen

Webbed feet are the best feet for swimming. The web opens to push hard against the water, like a frogman's flipper. When the foot comes back, the web closes so that the foot does not drag through the water. Coots spend a lot of time on land. They have partly webbed feet. Moorhens have hardly any webbing. They jerk their heads backwards and forwards when swimming.

Moulting

Female Mallard

Male Mallard

Ducks moult in late summer. The drake loses his colourful feathers and for a time looks rather like the female. New feathers have grown by early winter.

Chicks

Mallard

Young Mallards

New chicks are taken to the water by their mother. The chicks fall in and can swim straight away.

Gull

Mallard

When danger threatens Mallard chicks, the duck stretches out her neck and quacks loudly. The chicks dive to escape.

Great Crested Grebe

Great Crested Grebes are fish-eating water birds. The male and female both look after the young and carry their chicks on their backs.

Woodlands and Forests

All types of woods are good places for birds but you will see the bird most easily in places that are not too dark. Woods with open spaces or pools have more plants and insects for the birds to feed on.

The **Black Woodpecker** (46 cm) is the largest European Woodpecker. It is not found in Britain but breeds in other parts of Europe, mainly in coniferous forests.

The **Goldcrest** (9 cm) is the smallest European bird. It is often found in coniferous or mixed woods.

The **Chiffchaff** (11 cm) is smaller than a Sparrow and is a summer migrant from Africa. It is often found in deciduous woods and in young pine plantations.

CONIFEROUS FORESTS

The **Coal Tit** (11.5 cm) is only a little larger than a Goldcrest. It nests in coniferous forests.

BROADLEAVED WOODS

The **Green Woodpecker** (32 cm) is the same size as a domestic pigeon. It is frequently seen on the ground, feeding on ants, and is usually found in deciduous woods.

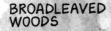

The **Nightingale** (16.5 cm) can often be heard singing in woods and forests but is rarely seen. It builds its nest among trees and bushes close to the ground.

The **Chaffinch** (15 cm) is a common bird, often found in broad-leaved woodlands and coniferous woods. In winter it prefers open land.

The **Woodcock** (34 cm) is found in deciduous woods where its plumage blends in perfectly with the dead leaves on the ground.

The **Lesser Spotted Woodpecker** (14.5 cm) is the smallest European Woodpecker. It is found in deciduous woods.

The **Nuthatch** (14 cm) feeds on nuts from hazel, beech and oak trees.

Woods with broad-leaved trees such as oak and beech contain many more birds than old pine forests or other coniferous forests. Young pine plantations and mixed woods which have many different kinds of trees in them, also have lots of birds.

The sizes given are beak-to-tail measurements.

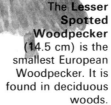

Food of Woodland Birds

IF IT IS WINDY, WATCH OUT FOR FALLING BRANCHES IN THE WOODS. TRY NOT TO STAND OR SIT NEAR TREES WHICH HAVE NESTS IN THEM. YOU MIGHT FRIGHTEN AWAY THE PARENT BIRDS

In autumn **Jays** collect the acorns from oak trees. They bury many of them and dig them up when they are short of food.

The **Tawny Owl** feeds on small animals like mice. It has very good eyesight and hearing and can catch its food even on the darkest nights.

Many birds, like the **Garden Warbler,** feed on caterpillars which are very common in woods.

The **Pied Flycatcher** catches insects by swooping down on them in a short flight from a lookout branch.

Holes in Trees

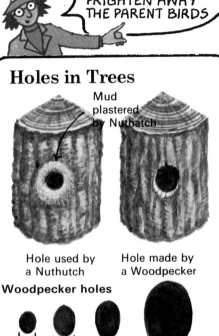

Mud plastered by Nuthatch

Hole used by a Nuthutch

Hole made by a Woodpecker

Woodpecker holes

4 cm. Lesser Spotted

4.5 cm. Greater Spotted

6.5 cm. Green

10 cm. Black

The different kinds of Woodpecker all make nesting holes in trees. These are sometimes used by other birds like the Nuthatch, or animals like bats and dormice.

Special Beaks

Hawfinch   Crossbill

Some birds like the Hawfinch and the Crossbill have special beaks for eating seeds.

Woodlands at Night

Many different kinds of owl live in woods. They range in size from the Pygmy Owl which is only 16.5 cm. high, to the

Eagle Owl, which can be as large as 71 cm.

These four owls are all drawn to the same scale

These three owls are all drawn to the same scale

Pygmy Owl

Scops Owl

Little Owl

Little Owl

Long-eared Owl

Tawny Owl

Eagle Owl

Nightjar

The Nightjar sleeps during the day, so is rarely seen. Its song can be heard after dark in summer.

Towns and Cities

You do not have to live in the country to be a birdwatcher. In the middle of towns you may only find Pigeons, Starlings and House Sparrows but where there are gardens and parks you will see many other kinds of birds. Some of these birds are quite used to people and can be very tame. This means that you will probably be able to get quite close to them and see them very clearly. The illustrations show some of the more common birds you might see in towns and cities.

The **Kestrel** is a town as well as a country bird. But the town Kestrel usually feeds on Sparrows instead of mice and beetles, and nests on high buildings instead of in trees.

1 Cliff Birds that Live in Towns

Black Redstart

Black Redstarts once nested on sea-cliffs and rocks. Now you are more likely to find them in towns. They build their nests on buildings.

The **Long-tailed Tit** is a hedge bird that can often be seen in parks and gardens. In autumn and winter family groups of about a dozen gather together.

The **Black-headed Gull** is one of the commonest town gulls. You will often see large numbers of them near reservoirs and gravel pits.

You will hardly ever see a **Swift** on the ground. It feeds and even sleeps as it is flying. At dusk you may see flocks of Swifts circling high above the roof-tops.

You will sometimes hear the warbling song of the **Skylark** as it flies high above parks and wasteland. In winter you may see flocks around gravel pits and sewage works.

Cities are surprisingly good places to look for birds. All birds need food and places to nest and sleep. Most gardens (3) and parks (2) have some trees and bushes where birds can nest and sleep without being disturbed by people. Many birds find perching places on buildings (5). Gulls fly out to sleep at gravel pits (1) or reservoirs (4) at night. Everywhere people spill or leave food on which birds can live. On the edge of cities birds find lots of food at sewage works (4), rubbish dumps(1). Railway

2

Rock Dove

Pigeons

The Pigeon is a relation of the Rock Dove, which nests on sea-cliffs. But the town Pigeon is now much more common than the Rock Dove and is often very tame. It feeds on bread and any other scraps it finds in parks or in the streets.

Noisy City Birds

Starling

Starlings are one of the commonest city birds and are usually found in huge, noisy flocks. In summer many of them move to the country.

House Martins build their mud nests under the roofs of many town houses.

Carrion Crows are quite common in parks and gardens.

Swallows look rather like House Martins but have longer tail feathers. You can often see them catching flies over rivers, gravel pits and sewage works.

Magpies are large black and white birds and are common in parks and gardens. They use twigs to build their nests in trees and tall hedges.

4

5

6

sidings and canals (6) where food is unloaded and often spilt are also good places for birds to find food, and have fewer people to disturb them. Many birds eat the seeds of weeds growing on waste ground and building sites. In winter, when there is little food in the countryside, many birds fly to the cities. There people put out food for them in parks and gardens.

Sea Coasts

The coast is always a good place for birds. In summer many birds fly to Europe from Africa and the Antarctic. They come to the shore to breed. In winter, small wading birds like the Knot come from the north to feed and wait for spring. Most of the cliff-nesting birds spend the winter far out at sea. Unfortunately, every year many birds lose their eggs and babies because people tread on the nests or stop the parent birds from feeding their young by frightening them away.

Waders' Beaks

Birds can find a lot of food on the beach. The shape of a wading bird's beak depends on the sort of food it eats. You can try to find out what the birds are eating by digging up the sand and looking for the food in it.

Avocet sifts for food

Curlew probes deeply

Dunlin picks food on and under the surface

Oystercatcher feeds on shellfish.

The Brent Goose is a rare winter visitor from Greenland or northern Russia where it breeds. It feeds on a plant called eelgrass which grows only on mudflats. It is the smallest wild goose.

Brent Goose

Shelduck

Shelduck

The Shelduck is one of the commonest large birds you will see on a salt marsh. It sometimes builds its nest in an old rabbit burrow.

Knot (summer plumage)

In winter large flocks of Knot fly south from their northern breeding grounds. They feed on sandy or muddy shores.

Common Tern

The Tern breeds on salt marshes, shingle or sandy shores. It builds its nest in a hollow in the ground.

Salt Marsh

Sandy Shore

Shingle Beach

Fish-Eaters' Beaks

Fish-eating birds do not all have the same kind of beak. The shape of the beak depends on the size and type of fish that the bird eats.

Common Tern

Razorbill

Gannet

Nesting Places

In winter cliffs are almost deserted but during the breeding season they are like large bird cities. The whole cliff is used for nesting. Each type of bird has its favourite spot for nesting.

Puffin

Puffins dig nesting burrows in the soil on the cliff-top. They use their huge, brightly coloured bills for digging and push away the soil with their webbed feet.

Gannet

The cliff-top is also the Gannet's favourite nesting place. Gannets nest in large numbers and build their untidy nests only about one metre apart from each other.

The Fulmar is a large silver-grey bird that spends most of its time out at sea. It looks rather like a gull but holds its wings straighter and stiffer when it is flying. It nests on rock ledges and sometimes on window ledges.

Razorbill

The Razorbill lays its one egg in cracks in the cliff or under rocks. The nest is sometimes a few pieces of seaweed but there is usually no proper nest at all.

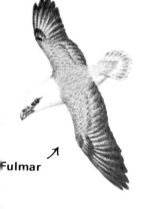

Fulmar

Guillemot

Like the Razorbill, the Guillemot makes no nest. It lays a single pear-shaped egg on a rock ledge. The shape of the egg helps to stop it rolling off. Guillemots nest in large numbers, crowded very close together.

The Cormorant's feathers are not waterproof, so when it leaves the water it often stands on a rock or post holding out its wings to dry. It builds a large untidy nest of seaweed and sticks in which it lays three or four eggs.

WATCH THE BIRDS AND TRY TO SEE WHAT THEY EAT. HOW DO THEY USE THEIR BEAKS WHEN FEEDING? HAVE THEY ANY SPECIAL WAY OF GETTING THEIR FOOD?

Cormorant

Cliffs

Shag

The Shag and the Cormorant are quite difficult to tell apart. The Shag is the smaller of the two and does not have the Cormorant's white face. In the breeding season it grows a little curly crest.

Mountains and Moorlands

Many of the birds that live on mountains and moorlands are well known because they are game-birds like the Grouse, or large and powerful birds of prey like the Buzzard or Golden Eagle. But you will see fewer birds here than by the coast or in woods because there is less food for them to eat. The smaller birds eat bilberries, the young shoots of heather and the seeds from mosses and grasses. The larger birds of prey feed mainly on small birds and animals.

The **Golden Eagle** is the largest bird that is found on moors and mountains. It is very rare in most parts of Europe.

The **Buzzard** is one of the commonest of the large birds of prey. It is similar to the Golden Eagle but is smaller and stubbier.

The **Short-eared Owl** nests on the ground. It often hunts in the daytime and feeds on small animals like voles and lemmings.

The **Raven** is the largest of the Crow family. It is even larger than the Buzzard. It flies slowly but powerfully and sometimes tumbles through the air.

The **Meadow Pipit** is the commonest small bird that you will see on moorland. It feeds on insects.

Willow Grouse

These two birds look different but are in fact very closely related. **The Red Grouse** is only found in Britain and the **Willow Grouse** only in Europe. The Willow Grouse is shown here in its partial winter plumage.

Red Grouse

Willow Grouse

Short-tailed Vole

EVERY YEAR PEOPLE GET LOST ON MOUNTAINS OR MOORS. MAKE SURE IT IS NOT YOU. NEVER GO ON YOUR OWN AND ALWAYS TELL SOMEONE WHERE YOU ARE GOING. KEEP TO PATHS AND WEAR WARM CLOTHES. MOUNTAINS CAN BE COLD EVEN IN SUMMER

An Underwater Fisher

The Dipper lives by fast-flowing mountain streams. It feeds on insects that it catches under the water.

Dipper

Shrikes

Shrikes (or Butcher Birds) have a habit of pinning their spare food such as bees, beetles and even small birds, onto branches or barbed wire. When food is scarce they may go back to collect it. The Redbacked Shrike is a rather rare summer visitor. The Great Grey Shrike breeds in Northern Europe and flies south in the winter.

Redbacked Shrike

Beetle

Great Grey Shrike

Changing Colour with the Seasons

Ptarmigan in summer

Ptarmigan in winter

The Ptarmigan can hide from its enemies because it always looks the same colour as the countryside. In summer its coat is mainly brown but in winter it turns pure white. It lives in the mountains of northern Europe.

The **Golden Plover** usually breeds on moors and hills. It lays its four eggs in a nest on the ground.

The **Wheatear** builds its nest in holes in walls and in old rabbit burrows.

The **Black Grouse** lives on the borders of moorland. The male (Blackcock) has a lyre-shaped tail.

The **Ring Ouzel** is a relative of the Blackbird and lives in remote mountain valleys.

Lemming (not found in Britain)

Migrating Birds

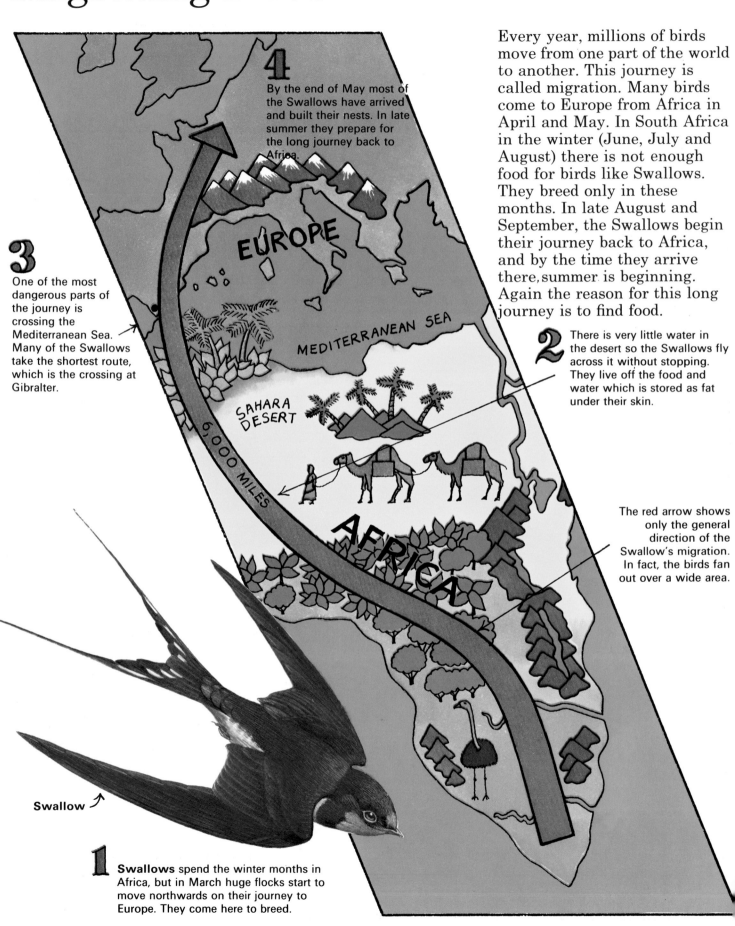

4 By the end of May most of the Swallows have arrived and built their nests. In late summer they prepare for the long journey back to Africa.

3 One of the most dangerous parts of the journey is crossing the Mediterranean Sea. Many of the Swallows take the shortest route, which is the crossing at Gibralter.

Every year, millions of birds move from one part of the world to another. This journey is called migration. Many birds come to Europe from Africa in April and May. In South Africa in the winter (June, July and August) there is not enough food for birds like Swallows. They breed only in these months. In late August and September, the Swallows begin their journey back to Africa, and by the time they arrive there, summer is beginning. Again the reason for this long journey is to find food.

2 There is very little water in the desert so the Swallows fly across it without stopping. They live off the food and water which is stored as fat under their skin.

EUROPE

MEDITERRANEAN SEA

SAHARA DESERT

9,000 MILES

AFRICA

The red arrow shows only the general direction of the Swallow's migration. In fact, the birds fan out over a wide area.

Swallow ↗

1 **Swallows** spend the winter months in Africa, but in March huge flocks start to move northwards on their journey to Europe. They come here to breed.

White Stork

Redwing

TRY TO KEEP A NOTE OF THE FIRST AND LAST DATES ON WHICH YOU SEE MIGRANT BIRDS. KEEP A RECORD OF THE WEATHER IN YOUR AREA DURING SPRING AND AUTUMN AND SEE IF THIS AFFECTS THE DATES ON WHICH BIRDS ARRIVE OR LEAVE

In some areas of Europe, flocks of large birds like the White Stork can be seen waiting by the coast. When the weather is good enough, they cross the sea and continue their migration.

The Redwing is a member of the Thrush family. In winter it flies south through Europe travelling mainly at night in large flocks.

Summer Visitors

Blackcap

Willow Warbler

These warblers are two of the commonest small birds that visit Europe in the summer. They come from Africa but in some winters a few Blackcaps stay in Europe.

Hoopoe

The Hoopoe, with its floppy flight, does not seem capable of flying far, but every autumn it flies to Africa and returns in spring.

Starling

Arctic Tern

Some birds fly even longer distances than the Swallow. One of these is the Arctic Tern. It flies from the Arctic, where it breeds, all the way to the southern tip of South America or South Africa. During the journey it stays mostly out at sea.

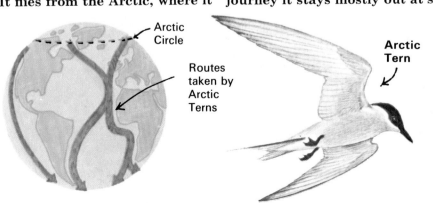

Arctic Circle

Routes taken by Arctic Terns

Arctic Tern

Many Starlings fly south in winter and are attracted to bright lights, such as lighthouses, at night. Many of them are killed by flying into buildings where they see lights.

Common Birds to Spot

Sparrow-sized Birds

The notes under each bird give its size from beak to tail. Each panel contains birds of a similar size. The coloured dots beside each bird tell you where to look for it and the red arrows show the points to look for.

- ● Water
- ● Woods
- ● Towns and Gardens
- ● Fields

The birds inside this panel are all drawn to the same scale.

Wren. 9.5 cm. Smallest bird you will see in gardens. Holds its tail cocked over its back.

Goldcrest. 9 cm. Smallest European bird. Feeds on insects and spiders.

Blue Tit. 11.5 cm. Only tit with blue head and wings. One of the most common garden birds.

Treecreeper. 12.5 cm. This mouse-like bird climbs trees.

Nuthatch. 14 cm. Has a long straight bill used for cracking open nuts.

Long-tailed Tit. 14 cm. Tail very long. Often seen in small flocks.

Great Tit. 14 cm. Has a black band down its belly.

Coal Tit. 11.5 cm. Has a white stripe on its neck.

Sand Martin. 12 cm. Has brown back and collar. Nests in holes in banks.

House Martin. 12.5 cm. Has a white rump and a shorter tail than the Swallow. Often nests in large groups.

Swallow. 19 cm. Has long tail feathers and a dark throat. Feeds on insects.

Swift. 16.5 cm. Has very long curved wings.

Blackbird-sized Birds

The birds inside this panel are all drawn to the same scale.

Starling. 21.5 cm. On the ground has an upright way of walking. Often seen in large flocks.

Blackbird. 25 cm. The male is all black with an orange beak. The female is brown with a brown beak.

Song Thrush. 23 cm. Both sexes look the same, with a brown back and spotted breast. Often feeds on snails.

Mistle Thrush. 27 cm. A greyer bird than the Song Thrush and the spots on the breast are larger and closer together.

Remember—if you cannot see a picture of the bird you want to identify on these pages, turn to the page earlier in the book which deals with the kind of place where you saw the bird.

Robin. 14 cm. Can be very tame. Has an orange breast.

Bullfinch. 14.5–16 cm. Has a black cap, white rump and short black bill.

Greenfinch. 14.5 cm. Has yellow wing bars and a greenish rump.

Goldfinch. 12 cm. Has a red face and a black and white head.

Dunnock. 14.5 cm. Feeds on the ground and moves slowly with a kind of creeping walk.

House Sparrow. 14.5 cm. A very common bird. The male has a grey and brown head and black throat.

Tree Sparrow. 14 cm. Has a brown head and a black spot on its white cheeks. Likes to nest in old trees.

Chaffinch. 15 cm. Has white wing bars and white outer tail feathers.

Kingfisher. 16.5 cm. Catches small fish for food.

The **Pied Wagtail** (18 cm.) lives in Britain, the **White** (18 cm.) in Europe.

Skylark. 18 cm. Has white outer tail feathers.

Yellowhammer. 16.5 cm. The male has a yellow head.

Linnet. 13.5 cm. The male has a red forehead and chest.

Great Spotted Woodpecker. 23 cm. Has large white wing patches and a black line from beak to neck.

Green Woodpecker. 32 cm. Has a bright red head and yellow rump. Often feeds on ants on the ground.

Cuckoo. 33 cm. Has a long tail. It lays its eggs in the nests of other birds.

Kestrel. 34 cm. The commonest falcon. Often seen hovering over fields before dropping onto its prey.

Remember—if you cannot see a picture of the bird you want to identify on these pages, turn to the page earlier in the book which deals with the kind of place where you saw the bird.

Crow-sized Birds

The birds inside this panel are all drawn to the same scale.

Collared Dove. 32 cm. Has a black half collar at the back of the neck.

Woodpigeon. 41 cm. Has a white patch on each side of the neck.

Buzzard. 51–56 cm. Has broad wings and tail. Plumage varies from pale to dark.

Barn Owl. 34 cm. A large white-looking owl. It hunts in twilight or at night. The remains of food can be found as pellets.

Lapwing. 30 cm. Has a thin crest and broad, black and white wings which show up when it is flying.

Breeding plumage (summer)

Herring Gull. 56–66 cm. Commonest gull on the coast. Has a large yellow beak with a red spot near the tip and grey wings.

Breeding plumage (summer)

Non-breeding plumage (winter)

Black-headed Gull. 35–38 cm. In winter, instead of a dark head, it has only a dark mark behind the eyes.

Mallard-sized Birds

The birds inside this panel are all drawn to the same scale.

Breeding plumage (summer)

Non-breeding plumage (winter)

Coot. 38 cm. Larger than a Moorhen. Is all black with a white beak and forehead. Likes large, open stretches of water.

Moorhen. 33 cm. Its beak is red and the underside of its tail white. Swims with a jerky movement.

Great Crested Grebe. 48 cm. The largest grebe. In summer, has brownish frills round the neck. In winter, blackish ear tufts.

←Female

Female

Male

Male

Tufted Duck. 43 cm. The most common diving duck. The male has a long drooping crest, the female is browner with a much smaller crest. Forms large flocks on lakes and reservoirs.

Mallard. 58 cm. The male has a green head, white collar and purple-brown breast. Both birds have a blue patch and white bars on their wings, which show up best in flight.

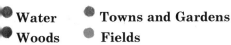

● Water ● Towns and Gardens
● Woods ● Fields

Hooded

Carrion

ackdaw. 33 cm. Has a grey ead and is smaller than the ll-black crows.

Magpie. 46 cm. A large bird with a long tail and black and white plumage.

The northern form of the **Carrion Crow** has black and grey feathers. It is called the **Hooded Crow** (47 cm.)

Rook. 46 cm. Has a thinner beak than the crow, with a bare white face.

Male

Female

Curlew. 51–58 cm. Largest wader. Has a long downward curved beak, a brown body, and long legs.

Pheasant. Male 66–89 cm. Female 53–63 cm. A large game-bird. The male is brightly coloured, the female browner with a shorter tail.

Larger Birds

These birds are not drawn to the same scale.

Whooper Swan

Juvenile Mute Swan

Female Mute Swan

Male Mute Swan

Bewick's Swan

Grey Heron. 90 cm. A large grey bird often seen standing at the water's edge. The nest is usually built in a tree.

Cormorant. 90 cm. Has a white chin and cheeks. Often seen sitting on rocks with its wings half-open.

Mute Swan. 152 cm. Has an orange bill with a black knob at the base. Swims with its neck curved.

Bewick's and Whooper Swan. 122 and 152 cm. Bewick's has a shorter bill with a smaller yellow patch. Both hold their necks stiffly when swimming.

Index

Avocet, **22**

Bearded Reedlings, **3**
Blackbird, 7, **10**, 15, **28**
Blackcap, **27**
Bullfinch, **10**, **29**
Bunting, Reed, **4**, **6**
Buzzard, **24**, **30**

Chaffinch, **10**, **18**, **29**
Chiffchaff, **18**
Coot, 15, **17**, **30**
Cormorant, **23**, **31**
Crossbill, **19**
Crow, 6-7; pellet, **9**; Carrion, **15**,
  21, **31**; Hooded, **31**
Cuckoo, **29**
Curlew, **6-7**, **22**, **31**; feather, **8**

Dipper, **25**
Dove, Collared, 15, **30**; Rock, **21**
Duck, Tufted, 16, **16**, **30**
Dunlin, **22**
Dunnock, **10**, 15, **29**

Eagle, Golden, **24**

Fulmar, **23**

Gannet, **23**
Goldcrest, **18**, **28**
Goldeneye, **17**
Goldfinch, **10**, **29**
Goose, **6**; Brent, **22**
Grebe, Great Crested, **17**, **30**
Greenfinch, 7, **10**, 15, **29**
Grouse, Black, **25**; Red, **24**;
  Willow, **24**
Guillemot, **23**
Gull, Black-Headed, 7, **20**, **30**;
  Herring, **30**; pellet, **9**

Hawfinch, **19**
Heron, **6-7**, 15, **16**; Grey, **31**;
  pellet, **9**
Hoopoe, **27**

Jackdaw, **31**; pellet, **8**
Jay, **19**; feather, **8**

Kestrel, **20**, **29**
Kingfisher, 15, **16**, **29**
Knot, **22**

Lapwing, 15, **30**
Linnet, **29**

Magpie, **6**, **21**, **31**; feather, **8**
Mallard, 15, 16-17, **16-17**, **30**
Martin, House, **13**, 15, **21**, **28**;
  Sand, 15, **28**
Moorhen, 15, **16-17**, **30**

Nightingale, 15, **18**
Nuthatch, **2**, 12, 15, **18**, **28**

Ouzel, Ring, **25**
Owl, Barn, **30**; Eagle, **19**; Little,
  19; Long-eared, **19**; Pygmy, **19**;
  Scops, **19**; Short-eared, **24**;
  Tawny, **19**; pellet, **9**

Oystercatcher, **22**; skull, **8**

Pheasant, 15, **31**
Pigeon, 20-1, **21**; Woodpigeon,
  15, **30**
Pintail, **16**
Pipit, Meadow, **24**
Plover, Golden, **25**
Ptarmigan, **25**
Puffin, **23**

Raven, **24**
Razorbill, **23**
Redstart, Black, **20**
Redwing, **27**
Robin, 7, **10**, 15, **29**
Rook, **15**, **31**

Sawbill, **16**
Shag, **23**
Shelduck, **22**
Shoveler, **17**
Shrike, Great Grey, **25**;
  Red-Backed, **25**
Siskin, **2**
Skylark, **20**, **29**
Sparrow, House, **10**, 12, 20, **29**;
  Tree, 12, **29**
Sparrowhawk, **6**; pellet, **8**
Starling, **10**, 12, 20, **21**, 27, **28**
Stonechat, **3**, **15**
Stork, White, **27**
Swallow, 15, **16**, **21**, **26**, **28**
Swan, Bewick's, **31**; Mute, **16**, **31**;
  Whooper, **31**
Swift, **20**, **28**

Tern, Arctic, **27**; Common, **22-3**;
  Sandwich (egg), **8**
Thrush, Mistle, **2**, **10**, 15, **28**;
  Song, **9**, **10**, **14**, 15, **28**
Tit, Blue, **10**, 12, **28**; Coal, 10, **18**,
  28; Great, **10**, 12, **28**; Long-
  Tailed, 15, **20**, **28**
Treecreeper, 7, **28**
Turnstone, **7**

Wagtail, Grey, **7**; Pied, **29**;
  White, **29**
Warbler, Willow, **27**
Wheatear, **25**
Wigeon, **16**

Woodcock, **18**
Woodpecker, **6**, 15; Black, **18**, **19**;
  Greater Spotted, 19, **29**;
  Green, **18**, 19, **29**; Lesser
  Spotted, **18**, 19
Wren, 12, 15, **28**

Yellowhammer, **29**

The name Usborne and the device are
Trade Marks of Usborne Publishing Ltd.

Books to Read

The *Oxford Book of Birds* and the
Pocket Oxford Book of Birds. Bruce
Campbell (OUP)
The *RSPB Guide to British Birds*
D. Saunders (Hamlyn)
The Book of British Birds (AA/Readers
Digest)
The *Observers' Book of Birds.* S. Vere
Benson (Warne)
**Older Readers may find the
following books helpful**
*A Field Guide to the Birds of Britain and
Europe.* R. T. Peterson, G. Mountford
and P. A. D. Hollom (Collins)
The 'New' Birdtable Book. Tony Soper
(David and Charles)
*Collins Guide to Animal Tracks and
Signs.* P. Bang, P. Dahlstrom (Collins)

Clubs and Societies

The national club for young birdwatchers
is the **Young Ornithologists' Club**.
Members receive their own magazine
Bird Life every other month and may
take part in competitions, projects and
local outings. The Club also organises
birdwatching holidays in many parts of
Britain. The YOC is the junior section of
the **Royal Society for the
Protection of Birds** and further
details may be obtained from The Lodge,
Sandy, Bedfordshire, SG19 2DL.
The British Trust for Ornithology
organises national surveys which are
carried out by volunteers, and
administers the ringing of birds. Junior
members must be aged 15.
Headquarters: Beech Grove, Tring,
Hertfordshire.

The Wildfowl Trust owns several reserves
for wildfowl and carries out important
research. For details about junior
membership write to: Membership
Secretary, The Wildfowl Trust, Slimbridge,
Gloucestershire.
**The Council for Environmental
Conservation** (address: Zoological
Gardens, Regent's Park, London NW1)
will supply the addresses of your local
Natural History Societies. (Send a
stamped self-addressed envelope for the
list.) Many of these have specialist
sections and almost all have field
meetings. **The Royal Society for Nature
Conservation** (address: 22 The Green,
Nettleham, Lincoln) will give you the
address of your local **County Naturalist
Trust,** which may have a junior branch.